ABRACADABRA
PERFORMANCE PIECES
TRUMPET

Published by Collins
An imprint of HarperCollins*Publishers* Ltd
The News Building
1 London Bridge Street
London
SE1 9GF

Browse the complete Collins catalogue at
www.collins.co.uk

© 2017 HarperCollins*Publishers* Ltd
ISBN 978-1-4729-2363-9

10 9 8 7 6 5 4 3 2 1

Printed in Great Britain by Martins the Printers.

Contents

CD tracks

For each piece, the first CD track listed is a complete performance track with live trumpet and the second is a backing track to play along with.

Duets have both Player 1 and Player 2 parts included in the performance track and neither part in the backing track. The backing tracks can be used by Player 1, Player 2, or both Players together.

L'Arlésienne Suite No. 1

performance 1   backing 2

Theme from Movement I: Prélude
Composed by Georges Bizet
Arranged by Christopher Hussey

Sarabande

performance · backing

from *Keyboard Suite in D minor*, HWV 437
Composed by George Frideric Handel
Arranged by Christopher Hussey

Slow and solemn

(violin cue)

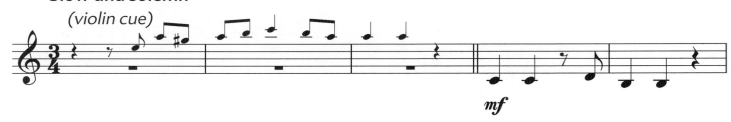

Stick dance (duet) | Player 1

from *Romanian Folk Dances*
Composed by Béla Bartók
Arranged by Christopher Hussey

performance 5   backing 6

(two-bar click in)

Stick dance (duet) Player 2

Spring song

from *Four Short Pieces for violin and piano*
Composed by Frank Bridge
Arranged by Christopher Hussey

D.S. al Coda   Coda

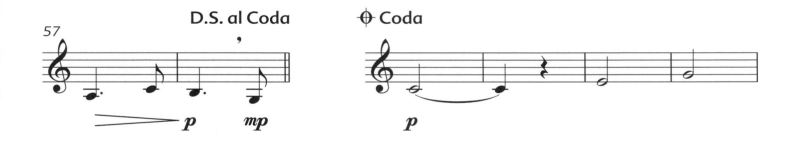

Symphony No. 40

Theme from Movement I
Composed by Wolfgang Amadeus Mozart
Arranged by Christopher Hussey

performance
9

backing
10

Hora mit tsibeles

Traditional Klezmer tune
Arranged by Christopher Hussey

Rondeau (duet) | Player 1

 performance 13
 backing 14

from *Abdelazer*
Composed by Henry Purcell
Arranged by Christopher Hussey

Rondeau (duet) Player 2

Pastime with good company

Composed by Anon. 16th century
Arranged by Christopher Hussey

Piano Trio

Theme from *Piano Trio in E♭ major*, Movement II
Composed by Franz Schubert
Arranged by Christopher Hussey

Et misericordia (duet) Player 1

performance **19** backing **20**

(two-bar click in)

from *Magnificat in D major*
Composed by Johann Sebastian Bach
Arranged by Christopher Hussey

Et misericordia (duet) Player 2

Lento

Tango

from *España*, Op. 165
Composed by Isaac Albéniz, orch. Leo Artok
Arranged by Christopher Hussey

performance · backing

Moderato, gracefully

The old castle

from *Pictures at an Exhibition*
Composed by Modest Mussorgsky, orch. Maurice Ravel
Arranged by Christopher Hussey

Largo

(bassoon cue)

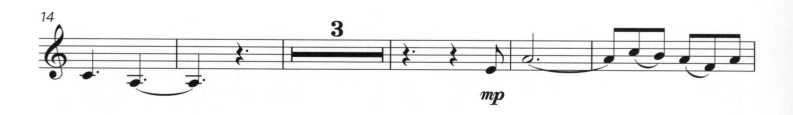

Chanson de matin (duet)

Composed by Edward Elgar
Arranged by Christopher Hussey

Player 1

performance 25 backing 26

(two-bar click in)

Chanson de matin (duet) Player 2

Danse macabre

Composed by Camille Saint-Saëns
Arranged by Christopher Hussey

performance 27 backing 28

Molto allegro
(violin cue)

1st: mp lightly
2nd: f lightly

mf broadly

mf marcato

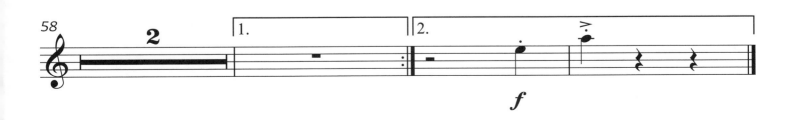

f

Recording

Backing tracks arranged and produced by Christopher Hussey

Trumpet played by Freddie Gavita

Performance recordings produced by Christopher Hussey

Book

Arrangements by Christopher Hussey

Cover design by Becky Chilcott

Design and music setting by Christopher Hussey

Edited by Flora Death

Printed in Great Britain by Martins the Printers.